T0199130

Hi, I'm Noah!

Written and Illustrated by
Emily Mae

FOR JASON, LILY, JJ AND LITTLE ROSIE

BE STRONG AND COURAGEOUS.
DO NOT BE AFRAID. DO NOT BE DISCOURAGED.
FOR THE LORD WILL BE WITH YOU WHEREVER YOU GO.

JOSHUA 1:9

WestBow Press books may be ordered through booksellers or by contacting:

WestBow Press
A Division of Thomas Nelson & Zondervan
1663 Liberty Drive
Bloomington, IN 47403
www.westbowpress.com
844-714-3454

Because of the dynamic nature of the Internet, any web addresses or links contained in this book may have changed since publication and may no longer be valid. The views expressed in this work are solely those of the author and do not necessarily reflect the views of the publisher, and the publisher hereby disclaims any responsibility for them.

Any people depicted in stock imagery provided by Getty Images are models, and such images are being used for illustrative purposes only. Certain stock imagery © Getty Images.

Interior Image Credit: Emily Mae

ISBN: 978-1-6642-7263-7 (sc)
ISBN: 978-1-6642-7265-1 (hc)
ISBN: 978-1-6642-7264-4 (e)

Library of Congress Control Number: 2022913266

Print information available on the last page.

WestBow Press rev. date: 08/12/2022

WestBow
PRESS®
A DIVISION OF THOMAS NELSON
& ZONDERVAN

Hi, my name is Noah.
I have three sons and a wife.
I was 600 years old
when God changed my whole life.

1

Long ago, when the earth was young,
God saw all the people were bad.
And even though God loved them so,
this made him very sad.

But, there was one who loved God back
and was seen as good in God's eyes.
His name just happened to be Noah
and he was very, very wise.

HI THERE! IT'S ME AGAIN.

God had planned to flood the world,
but Noah and the animals made Him smile.
He decided to cover whole earth with water,
but only for a short little while.

God told Noah to build an ark
and left all the animals in his care.
So Noah built a boat big enough
for each and every pair.

5

Noah listened as he always did
and made the boat from gopherwood.
For Noah knew God believed in him,
so he always knew he could.

Two of every animal
each made their way.
From the smallest to the tallest,
the number grew every day.

Noah said to all the people
"Come repent and stay dry".
And even though they laughed at him,
he knew he had to try.

Noah made sure his family
was safe upon the boat.
He counted and checked all the animals
down to the very last goat.

Then it rained for weeks and weeks
without an end in sight.
But Noah had faith in God
and prayed with all his might.

The waters rose and the winds howled,
but the ark was big and strong.
As long as they had faith in God,
Noah knew nothing would go wrong.

Before long the earth was flooded
and Noah could see no land.
Yet, after forty days the rain did stop,
just as God had planned.

The waters flooded the earth
as one hundred and fifty days went by.
But God remembered the animals and Noah
and sent a wind to make the land dry.

So Noah asked his friend, the Dove,
"Please fly and look for dry land".
After a time the dove came back
dropping an olive branch in his hand.

All was quiet in the world.
Nothing made a sound.
They looked and looked for a sign of land,
but nothing could be found.

The dove set off again,
waiting until the seventh day.
And when the dove did not return,
Noah knew he had found the way.

Noah thanked God for keeping them safe
And as the earth began to dry,
God promised to never again flood the world,
which He sealed with a rainbow in the sky.

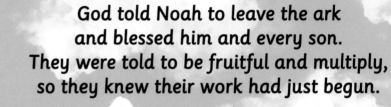

God told Noah to leave the ark
and blessed him and every son.
They were told to be fruitful and multiply,
so they knew their work had just begun.

The animals got off the boat as well,
and journeyed far and wide.
They covered all the earth again
and God smiled down with pride.

Now when the clouds part
and you see a rainbow above,
this is a reminder of God's promise
and his unconditional love.

20

Noah's Prayer

God,
Help me listen when You speak. Help my
follow Your instructions and obey, even when
it is hard. Thank You for always keeping Your
promises and sending a rainbow to remind us
of Your love.
Amen

We learned from Noah that God speaks to us and if we listen and have faith, we can never go wrong.

GOD KEEPS HIS PROMISES.

Noahs Song
(Itsy bitsy melody)

The animals went in the ark just as God had planned.
Down came the rain and covered all the land.
Out came the sunshine and dried up all the rain, and the rainbow reminds us of God's promise to Noah again.

Printed in the United States
by Baker & Taylor Publisher Services